1 MONTH OF
FREE
READING

at
www.ForgottenBooks.com

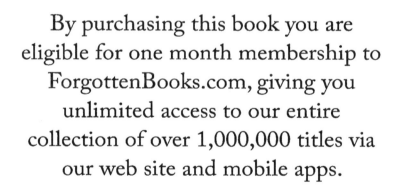

By purchasing this book you are eligible for one month membership to ForgottenBooks.com, giving you unlimited access to our entire collection of over 1,000,000 titles via our web site and mobile apps.

To claim your free month visit:
www.forgottenbooks.com/free947425

ISBN 978-0-260-42478-5
PIBN 10947425

Historic, archived document

Do not assume content reflects current
scientific knowledge, policies, or practices.

Foreign Crops and MARKETS

VOLUME 58   NUMBER 12

Summaries:

TOBACCO (Page 226)

CHICKENS

and

EGGS (Page 229)

ALMONDS (Page 235)

CONTENTS

FOR RELEASE

MONDAY

MARCH 21, 1949

Issued by the OFFICE OF FOREIGN AGRICULTURAL RELATIONS
UNITED STATES DEPARTMENT OF AGRICULTURE, WASHINGTON, D.C.

L A T E   N E W S

After long delay, the security price for the 1948 Greek currant crop has been fixed at 2,300 drachmas per oka (8.1 cents per pound), and for sultana raisins at 2,750 drachmas per oka (9.7 cents per pound). Growers were dissatisfied with these low prices, especially since they were set so late in the season.

- - - - - -

The British Board of Trade has announced that as of March 7 it has granted an open general license which permits the following nuts to be imported without restrictions: chestnuts and walnuts in shell consigned from France; chestnuts, filberts and walnuts in shell, from Italy; almonds, chestnuts and filberts in shell, from Spain, and filberts in shell, from Turkey.

- - - - - -

Reports from Shanghai state that 17,380 bales (500 pounds gross) of cotton arrived at that port in February 1949 as compared to only 5,670 bales in January. Arrivals of imported cotton at Shanghai for the first 7 months of the current season (beginning August 1, 1948) were reported at 105,000 bales, of which 58,700 bales were from the United States and 46,300 bales from India. Deliveries to mills of imported cotton from stocks in port amounted to 63,700 bales during the month of February 1949. Port stocks on February 28, 1949, at Shanghai were reported at 125,000 bales, of which 96,000 bales were aid cotton from the United States.

- - - - - -

The Government of Pakistan, after consultation with representatives of the Government of India, has decided not to enforce the lapsing clause in regulations regarding cotton purchased for export to India during the first quota period but not shipped prior to February 28. (See Foreign Crops and Markets, March 14, 1949.) The validity of licenses which would have expired on that date is extended through May 15, 1949. Licenses for the balance--350,000 Pakistan bales--of the 1948-49 quota of 650,000 bales (542,000 bales of 500 pounds) will be issued immediately, valid for shipment through August 31.

FOREIGN CROPS AND MARKETS

Published weekly to inform producers, processors, distributors and consumers of farm products of current developments abroad in the crop and livestock industries, foreign trends in prices and consumption of farm products, and world agricultural trade. Circulation of this periodical is free, but restricted to those needing the information it contains for the conduct of their production, marketing, educational, news dissemination and other related activities. Issued by the Office of Foreign Agricultural Relations of the United States Department of Agriculture, Washington 25, D. C.

WORLD FLUE-CURED TOBACCO PRODUCTION DECLINES

World production of flue-cured tobacco for the year beginning July 1, 1948 is estimated at 1,805 million pounds, which is a decline of 77 million pounds or about 4 percent from the record production of 1,882 million pounds in 1947-48. It is also slightly smaller than the large 1946-47 crop of 1,832 million pounds, but it is 46 percent above the 1935-36 through 1939-40 annual average of 1,238 million pounds.

Increased world demand for flue-cured leaf has encouraged larger plantings in most producing countries. Since the war there has been a decided shift in consumer demand from dark and cigar tobaccos to flue-cured and certain other light types used principally in cigarettes. The world effective demand for flue-cured tobacco and especially United States flue-cured would be considerably greater if it were not for the general shortage of dollar exchange, and trade restrictions by the principal tobacco importing countries.

United States. The 1948 flue-cured crop was 18 percent below the 1947 outturn, according to the latest official estimate. A production of 1,081 million pounds was obtained from 882,800 acres. The 1948 yield of 1,225 pounds per acre was the highest on record and is attributed to heavy applications of fertilizer, close planting and generally favorable growing conditions. The 1948 production was 25 percent above the prewar (1935-39) average. The crop was 60 percent of the world total flue-cured production, compared with the prewar (1935-39) average of 70 percent.

Flue-cured acreage allotments in 1948 were reduced by approximately 27 percent, because of the unfavorable outlook for exports, particularly to the United Kingdom which is the largest importer of United States flue-cured leaf. United Kingdom purchases of 1948 crop flue-cured leaf totaled only about 60 million pounds compared with normal purchases of approximately 200 million pounds.

Canada. Flue-cured production in Canada in 1948 totaled about 100 million pounds from 90,874 acres, as compared with 87 million pounds from 103,694 acres in 1947. The 1948 crop was 15 percent greater than in 1947, but 16 percent below the record 1946 crop of 119 million pounds. The increase over 1947 was a result of more favorable weather during the growing season than was the case in 1947. During the 5 years 1935-39 production of flue-cured leaf in Canada averaged 55 million pounds annually.

Brazil. The 1948-49 flue-cured crop is estimated at about 47 million pounds from 38,103 acres, compared with about 41 million pounds from 34,347 acres in 1947-48. Heavy demands from domestic manufacturers leaves little or no flue-cured tobacco available for export. In recent years, flue-cured plantings in Brazil, chiefly in the States of Rio Grande do Sul and Santa Catarina, have increased sharply.

FLUE-CURED TOBACCO: Acreage and production in specified countries, 1948 with comparisons a/

Country	Acreage				Production			
	Average 1935-39	1946	1947	1948 (Preliminary)	Average 1935-39	1946	1947	1948 (Preliminary)
	acres	acres	acres	acres	1,000 pounds	1,000 pounds	1,000 pounds	1,000 pounds
Canada	50,703	91,432	103,694	90,874	54,616	119,027	86,863	100,195
Mexico	c/	c/	c/	c/	b/ 800	3,300	2,900	2,300
United States	981,400	1,188,800	1,161,200	882,800	863,620	1,352,024	1,317,466	1,081,034
Italy	c/	4,660	c/	7,413	2,846	7,150	12,000	14,109
China	132,300	c/	214,000	380,000	150,900	100,000	143,000	270,000
Manchuria	10,540	c/	c/	c/	13,930	15,000	15,000	c/
India	b/ 67,000	127,109	132,930	130,000	31,280	58,650	71,000	c/
Taiwan (Formosa)	1,988	c/	c/	9,700	3,235	733	6,800	8,000
Korea	7,674	30,000	54,000	57,000	11,839	6,200	12,800	19,000
Argentina	b/ 955	c/	c/	7,289	b/ 913	7,165	6,929	6,482
Brazil	c/	27,675	34,347	38,103	c/	32,716	41,050	47,364
Nyasaland	c/	c/	c/	c/	2,574	3,000	2,600	2,500
Southern Rhodesia	48,010	91,800	116,172	c/	24,623	57,918	76,000	c/
Union of South Africa	c/	c/	c/	c/	4,996	19,700	24,578	20,000
Australia	9,913	4,492	4,203	4,335	5,276	3,994	2,378	3,035
New Zealand	1,740	3,700	4,110	4,130	1,370	3,440	4,485	5,255
Estimated production in all other countries d/	78,000	226,000	154,000	247,000	65,032	42,399	56,544	225,758
Estimated Total	1,390,723	1,795,668	1,978,656	1,858,644	1,237,855	1,832,416	1,882,393	1,805,032

a/ Year beginning July 1. For north temperate zone countries, harvests July through October of the year shown; for all other countries, harvests January through June of the following year. This represents a change from previous summaries of world production of flue-cured tobacco which combined July through October harvests in north temperate zone countries with harvests in other countries January through June of the same calendar year. b/ Less than five year average. c/ Data not available. d/ Includes approximations for countries not listed and for countries listed where data are not available.

China. The 1948 flue-cured crop is estimated at about 270 million
pounds from 380,000 acres, compared with 143 million pounds from
214,000 acres in 1947. The 1948 crop was the largest ever produced
in China; it was almost double that of 1947 and exceeds the 1935-39
annual average by about 120 million pounds. Flue-cured tobacco is
produced in the Provinces of Honan, Shantung, Anhwei, Yunnan,
Kweichow and Szechuan. It is reported that much of the 1948 crop
will not reach manufacturing centers because of disruptions in the
transportation system. It is also understood that a substantial part
of the crop was air-cured rather than flue-cured. As a result of
these factors, China will probably need to make substantial imports
of flue-cured leaf this year if cigarette production is maintained.

Other Far Eastern Countries. Total production of flue-cured tobacco
in Manchuria, Taiwan (Formosa), Korea, Japan, Thailand (Siam) and
India is estimated at 167 million pounds. According to preliminary
reports Korea's 1948 crop totaled 19 million pounds, compared with
12.8 million pounds in 1947 and an annual average of 11.8 million
pounds in the 1935-39 period. Taiwan's 1948 crop is placed at 8
million pounds, compared with 6.8 million pounds in 1947 and an annual
average of 3.2 million pounds in the 1935-39 period. For the other
Asiatic countries production in 1948-49 is estimated to be somewhat
greater than in 1947-48 and considerably above the 5-year average;
however, definite information on production in these countries is not
available.

Other Countries. The Union of South Africa's flue-cured production
is estimated at 20 million pounds, or a decrease of 19 percent from
1947-48. Southern Rhodesia hoped to produce about 90 million pounds
of flue-cured tobacco this year, but due to unfavorable weather and
a shortage of labor it is now anticipated that total production will
be substantially below this figure. Argentina's 1948-49 crop is
placed at 6.5 million pounds, or slightly smaller than in 1947-48.
Italy produced about 14.1 million pounds in 1948, or about 18 percent more than in 1947. Other countries producing some flue-cured
tobacco include Mexico, Nyasaland, Northern Rhodesia, British East
Africa, Venezuela, El Salvador, Nicaragua, Spain, Mauritius,
Australia, and New Zealand.

This is one of a series of regularly scheduled reports on world
agricultural production, approved by the Office of Foreign Agricultural
Relations Committee on Foreign Crop and Livestock Statistics. For
this report, the committee was composed of Joseph A. Becker, Chairman,
C. M. Purves, J. Barnard Gibbs, C.E. Pike, Constance H. Farnworth, and
Mary L. E. Jones.

WORLD EGG PRODUCTION IN 1948, CURRENT CHICKEN NUMBERS

Egg production in the principal producing countries of the world in 1948 was about 1.3 percent above the 1947 level. Nearly all the increase occurred in western Europe where the recovery in poultry numbers has been rapid, considering the short grain supply from the 1947 harvest. Egg output in Canada dropped in 1948 but in the United States it was maintained at the 1947 level although materially below the peak wartime level.

Chicken numbers at the beginning of 1949 equalled or exceeded prewar numbers in the United Kingdom, France, Sweden and Spain. Satisfactory progress was made in Italy and Belgium. Rebuilding of flocks has been slower in the Netherlands, Norway and to a lesser extent in Denmark. These countries are considerably dependent upon imported grains and feedstuffs.

Much of the increase in egg production and in poultry numbers in Europe reflected increases in the number and size of small flocks. Commercial or specialized poultry flocks increased less because of the limited availability of commercial feeds. Small producers with a few hectares of land found it profitable to convert their home-grown feeds into chickens and eggs. These small producers, including a considerable number of self-suppliers, could meet their delivery quotas at controlled prices, where in effect, and market their surplus on the open market at highly profitable prices.

The delivery of eggs by producers and the rationing of supplies to consumers continue in deficit countries such as Austria, Czechoslovakia and Norway. Rationing has been suspended temporarily in the United Kingdom during the current flush producing months. In France, Italy, Spain, Sweden and Belgium controls were previously lifted.

With a somewhat better feed situation since the 1948 harvest, together with a strong demand for eggs and poultry as a palatable food and as a substitute for red meats, the production of poultry and eggs in most European countries will expand in 1949. Supplies of red meats in 1949 and 1950 will still be short and production of eggs and poultry will continue to be profitable.

The rate-of-lay in most European countries has shown some improvement, notwithstanding an unsatisfactory general feed situation. Apparently, producers are finding that their chickens respond well to increases in feed and are directing their feeds to this enterprise, possibly at the expense of other uses. Furthermore, a low capital outlay is required, plus the quick expected returns.

In many of the European countries, steps have been taken to improve the producing qualities of chickens. Improved stock is imported and government breeding stations are maintained to distribute hatching eggs and chicks to producers at reasonable prices. Considerable further improvement in the producing qualities of chickens can be expected in the immediate future. This improvement will not reduce the size of

CHICKENS: Number in specified countries, average 1934-38,
annual 1946-1949

Countries	Date applicable	Average 1934-38	1946	1947	1948	1949
		Thousands	Thousands	Thousands	Thousands	Thousands	Thousands
North America						
Canada...............	1/ Dec. 1	44,077	51,697	54,728	47,310	40,000
Guatemala...............		2/ 664	-	-	-	-
Mexico...............	March	3/ 36,368	-	-	-	-
Newfoundland and						
Labrador............		4/ 387	371	377	-	-
Panama...............		2/ 195	1,372	1,528	-	-
United States...........	Jan. 1	408,177	530,203	474,441	461,550	448,838
Cuba...............	July	-	10,500	10,000	9,000	8,500
Dominican Republic.....		2,358	1,906	1,900	-	-
Europe						
Albania...............		2,060	1,800	-	-	-
Austria...............	1/ Dec. 3	2/ 8,862	5,300	5,400	5,800	5,600
Belgium...............	1/ Dec. 31	16,500	11,111	13,333	13,500	16,100
Bulgaria...............	1/ Dec. 31	5/ 11,814	-	-	-	-
Czechoslovakia.........	May 27	2/ 31,875	-	6/ 10,660	6/ 11,982	6/ 14,978
Denmark...............	July	2/ 27,643	18,388	19,415	23,816	26,000
Eire...............	June	15,961	15,263	14,537	-	-
Finland 7/...........	Sept. 1	2,853	1,171	-	-	-
France 8/...........	1/ Fall	145,000	-	145,500	-	-
Germany...............	1/ Dec.	86,624	9/ 39,018	-	-	-
Greece 10/...........	1/ Nov. 30	11,679	8,200	7,500	8,200	-
Hungary...............	Feb. 28	5/ 17,880	11/16,000	-	-	-
Italy...............		76,000	-	12/50,613	-	-
Luxembourg.............	1/ Dec. 1	2/ 515	275	350	380	433
Netherlands...........	June	29,632	13/ 3,078	13/ 7,315	-	13/ 9,843
Norway...............	June 20	5,686	2,926	3,768	4,663	5,500
Poland and Danzig.....	July	50,000	20,000	-	39,000	-
Portugal...............	1/ Dec. 31	14/ 5,716	-	-	-	-
Rumania...............		2/ 31,853	15/10,939	-	-	-
Spain...............	July 1	16/28,972	17/22,468	-	37,200	33,500
Sweden...............	Sept. 16	10,980	-	18/12,395	18/13,991	18/15,000
Switzerland...........	Apr.	5,544	5,043	5,025	-	-
United Kingdom - Farm..	June	73,402	60,576	64,880	79,200	91,000
Total..	June	-	76,393	81,526	-	-
Yugoslavia.............	1/ Dec. 31	18,021	-	-	-	-
Asia						
Lebanon...............	1/ Dec.	-	1,400	1,450	-	-
Palestine...............		2/ 1,914	-	-	-	-
Syria...............		1,525	2,029	1,826	1,900	-
Turkey...............		16,794	18,422	18,514	17,303	-
China...............		265,765	184,984	204,115	-	-
Japan...............	July	51,094	19,000	-	-	-
India...............		-	146,081	-	-	-
Pakistan...............		-	44,732	-	-	-
Philippine Islands.....		25,365	9,434	-	23,000	25,000
South America						
Argentina.............	June	19/42,988	-	-	-	-
Brazil...............		14/ 59,000	-	-	60,000	-
Chile...............	June	2/ 1,026	5,000	4,500	3,600	-
Paraguay...............		-	-	2,000	-	-
Uruguay...............		19/ 4,814	-	-	-	-
Africa						
Egypt...............	July	14/26,889	-	-	-	-
French Morocco.........		2/ 50,000	-	-	-	-
Union of South Africa..	Aug	19/14,000	18,600	16,000	-	-
Oceania						
Australia...............	1/ Dec. 31	15,541	15,000	-	-	-
New Zealand...........	March	14/ 3,489	-	-	-	-

1/End of year estimates (October to December) included under the following year for comparison. Thus, for Canada, the December 1, 1946 estimate of 51,697 is shown under 1946. 2/ Average for 2 to 4 years only. 3/ 1940. 4/ 1938. 5/ 1935. 6/ January 1. 7/ Adult poultry. 8/ Represents chickens raised. 9/ Four zones. 10/ All poultry. 11/ September. 12/ Hens and cocks. 13/ December previous year; hens and pullets. 14/ 1936. 15/ 58 countries instead of 71 as for prewar. 16/ 1939. 17/ April. 18/ June. 19/ 1937.

Office of Foreign Agricultural Relations. Prepared or estimated on the basis of official statistics of foreign governments, reports of United States Foreign Service officers, results of office research and other information. Data relate to prewar boundaries, unless otherwise noted.

EGGS: Number produced 1/ in specified countries, average 1934-38, annual 1945-48

Countries	Average 1934-38	1945	1946	1947	1948
	Millions	Millions	Millions	Millions	Millions
North America					
Canada................	2,638	—	3,883	4,484	4,214
Panama................	—	—	—	52	—
United States.........	35,498	55,858	55,590	55,252	55,168
Cuba..................	320	324	300	288	276
Dominican Republic....	—	—	60	60	—
Europe					
Albania...............	143	—	—	—	—
Austria...............	663	336	270	285	350
Belgium...............	1,693	400	1,100	1,380	1,440
Bulgaria..............	682	273	—	—	—
Czechoslovakia........	1,958	596	776	903	1,110
Denmark...............	1,979	858	883	995	1,568
Eire..................	1,086	760	801	733	880
Finland...............	317	—	93	117	—
France................	6,200	—	6,200	6,300	6,100
Germany...............	6,585	—	—	—	—
Greece................	550	332	352	331	—
Hungary...............	1,050	66	110	—	—
Italy.................	5,600	2,400	3,600	4,300	4,600
Luxembourg............	40	—	—	30	35
Netherlands...........	1,978	200	385	914	1,000
Norway................	369	86	155	198	263
Poland and Danzig.....	3,500	—	2,276	—	—
Portugal..............	250	—	—	—	—
Rumania...............	1,500	—	2/ 532	—	—
Spain.................	1,700	—	—	1,992	1,800
Sweden................	900	970	1,149	1,217	1,335
Switzerland...........	423	250	300	330	—
United Kingdom-Farm 3/	4/ 3,871	2,090	2,418	2,600	3,000
Total...	4/ 5,098	3,409	3,850	4,000	4,300
Yugoslavia............	1,000	—	—	—	—
Asia					
Lebanon...............	—	65	65	—	—
Palestine.............	108	150	200	—	—
Syria.................	92	105	120	90	110
Turkey................	1,003	851	863	895	—
Japan.................	3,553	864	936	—	—
Philippine Islands....	—	—	—	—	250
South America					
Argentina.............	1,127	—	—	—	2,160
Brazil................	—	—	520	460	370
Chile.................	—	—	—	100	—
Paraguay..............	—	—	—	—	—
Uruguay...............	289	—	358	326	—
Africa					
Egypt.................	751	—	—	—	—
French Morocco........	1,000	—	—	444	—
Union of South Africa.	5/	480	—	372	—
Oceania					
Australia 6/..........	708	1,358	1,470	1,431	1,440
New Zealand...........	430	—	—	—	—

1/ Relates to farm production in Canada and the United States, but data for many countries not explicit on this point. 2/ 58 countries. 3/ Year ending in May of year indicated. 4/ 3-year average. 5/ Not available. 6/ Commercial production.

Office of Foreign Agricultural Relations. Prepared or estimated on the basis of official statistics of foreign governments, reports of United States Foreign Service officers, results of office research, and other information. Data relate to prewar boundaries, unless otherwise noted.

flock needed to maintain egg consumption per capita, as it will be offset by the increase in the human population in European countries.

Although Denmark was able to export some eggs in the immediate postwar years, the trade in eggs between countries in Europe is only now showing sizable gains. Belgium, Netherlands, Poland, Hungary, Yugoslavia and Eire are beginning to resume their exports.

The farm production of eggs in Canada in 1948 fell to 4.2 billion compared with a peak level of nearly 4.5 billion in 1947. A sharp liquidation of chickens occurred in the fall of 1947 because of short feed supplies and the resulting unfavorable egg-feed price relationship. The 1948 hatch was smaller and the number of layers was 23 percent fewer in December 1948, and 21 percent fewer in January 1949, compared with a year earlier. The reduction in the number of layers was partially offset in December by a higher rate-of-lay but more severe weather in January 1949 than in January 1948 pulled the rate-of-lay down 2 percent. Thus, 1949 was started off with a net egg production of 23 percent below the initial month in 1948.

Chickens on farms in the United States on January 1, 1949 were 3 percent fewer than a year earlier and 6 percent below the 10-year average. Fewer chickens were raised in 1948 but farmers retained a larger-than-usual proportion of the pullets raised. Egg production in the United States in 1948 was only slightly below the 1947 output. With lower feed costs and increased feed availability, heavier feeding, together with mild weather, is currently resulting in a high rate-of-lay, and egg production in 1949 may slightly exceed 1948, although there were fewer hens and pullets at the beginning of the year.

In the Eastern Mediterranean countries the demand for eggs and poultry has increased interest in this industry. Feed supplies have been available for some expansion. As indicated by the wholesale receipts at the 7 important consuming centers in the Union of South Africa, egg production and poultry numbers have increased since 1947. Feed supplies have been favorable and the increase in the production of eggs has permitted some exports of eggs to the United Kingdom.

Chicken numbers in Australia on March 31, 1948 were lower because of a shortage of suitable feedstuffs in 1947. Higher current costs of feed and other items used by the industry are tending to reduce the number of chickens and the output of eggs. While the reduction is not expected to be large, information available indicates that Australian egg production may level off slightly below the peak level reached in the 1946-47 season.

(Continued on Page 249)

1948 MID-SEASON ALMOND REPORT 1/

The 1948 preliminary estimate of shelled almond production in the 6 leading foreign commercial producing countries is 57,600 short tons (revised) compared with 77,500 tons in 1947, and 71,700 tons in 1946. The estimate is 12 percent smaller than the 5-year (1942-46) average of 65,200 tons, and 13 percent smaller than the 10-year (1937-46) average of 66,300 tons. The small crop in Italy, the world's largest producer of shelled almonds, reduced the world total. In Spain production early in the season was estimated slightly above average, then well below average; but at mid-season, when better information became available, it was found to have been only slightly below average.

It is still somewhat too early to forecast the probable 1949 crop. However, blossoming has been in progress in all countries and should be completed by the end of this month. All available information indicates no adverse weather has been experienced thus far. However, the danger of late frosts and strong winds is not yet over. Growers in all countries believe a good crop will be harvested this fall. The Italian crop is expected to be much larger than that of 1948.

The stocks remaining at mid-season from the 1948, and earlier harvests, is tentatively estimated at 41,000 short tons, shelled basis, or about 71 percent of the estimated production in 1948. There was a substantial carry-over from the 1947 harvest at the start of the season. The present stocks represent about 50 percent of the estimated total available supply at the start of the season. The largest stocks are 20,000 short tons in Spain, followed by 16,000 tons in Italy. There are an estimated 500 tons in France, and the balance is about evenly distributed between Portugal and Iran. The bulk of the tonnage available as usual is still in growers' hands.

The 1948-49 marketing season to date, as far as exports are concerned, is still far from a normal prewar season. The continued absence from the international market of Germany, the largest prewar market for almonds, is one of the principal reasons for such abnormally heavy mid-season stocks. The slow economic recovery of many European countries has kept exports at relatively low levels. Unfortunately, official export statistics of the producing countries are not available and this prevents an accurate check of the international movement of this commodity. On the basis of trade estimates, Italy has had the best export season of the 6 countries. Italian prices and quality have been the most attractive. United States imports for consumption of Italian shelled almonds for the period September-January were 2,883 tons, of total imports of 3,192 tons from all sources. In addition, according to declared exports, another 553 tons were exported to the United States in February. United States imports of Spanish almonds stopped in November because of the countervailing duties assessed on Spanish nuts.

1/ A more extensive statement can be obtained from the Office of Foreign Agricultural Relations.

ALMONDS, SHELLED: Estimated commercial production in specified countries, 1948 with comparisons

Year	France	French Morocco	Iran	Italy	Portugal	Spain	Foreign total	United States
				Rounded to nearest 100 short tons				
				Short tons				
Average								
1942-46	700:	1,800:	6,400:	28,400:	2,400:	25,500:	65,200:	26,100
1937-46	700:	2,400:	7,100:	29,500:	2,600:	24,000:	66,300:	20,500
Annual								
1930	400:	1,100:	1/	34,000:	1,800:	22,200:2/	59,500:	13,500
1931	900:	2,600:	1/	17,000:	3,800:	26,600:2/	50,900:	14,800
1932	1,300:	2,100:	1/	28,000:	1,700:	20,600:2/	53,700:	14,000
1933	1,700:	2,600:	1/	33,000:	3,300:	24,600:2/	65,200:	12,900
1934	1,700:	1,800:	1/	34,300:	3,000:	29,600:2/	70,400:	10,900
1935	1,300:	700:	7,400:	33,400:	1,900:	26,200:	70,900:	9,300
1936	500:	1,800:	4,000:	33,500:	1,100:	25,100:	66,000:	7,600
1937	900:	3,600:	6,300:	33,000:	1,400:	20,100:	66,000:	20,000
1938	500:	3,100:	11,000:	44,000:	3,500:	24,000:	86,100:	15,000
1939	200:	4,900:	8,800:	15,000:	7,000:	20,000:	55,900:	21,600
1940	800:	2,200:	8,800:	28,600:	2,200:	24,700:	67,300:	12,000
1941	700:	1,600:	4,400:	31,900:	200:	24,200:	63,000:	6,000
1942	800:	1,600:	5,300:	14,500:	2,000:	27,000:	51,200:	23,800
1943	600:	1,100:	7,000:	21,400:	2,100:	29,000:	61,200:	17,500
1944	1,000:	600:	5,300:	22,700:	1,700:	20,900:	52,200:	24,000
1945	500:	3,300:	6,600:	50,600:	2,300:	26,400:	89,700:	27,200
1946	700:	2,400:	7,700:	33,000:	3,700:	24,200:	71,700:	37,800
1947 3/	1,000:	1,200:	6,000:	46,200:	1,100:	22,000:	77,500:	29,200
1948 3/	:4/ 1,100:	3,300:	7,700:	18,700:	2,900:4/	23,900:4/	57,600:	29,600

1/ Not available.
2/ Excluding Iran.
3/ Preliminary.
4/ Revised.

Office of Foreign Agricultural Relations. Prepared or estimated on the basis of official statistics of foreign governments, reports of United States Foreign Service officers, results of office research, and other information.

UNITED STATES: Imports for consumption of shelled and unshelled almonds, from specified countries, 1947-48, with comparisons.

Season, September through August

Year	French Morocco	Italy	Portugal	Spain	Other countries	Total
			Short tons			
Shelled						
Average:						
1942-46	16	712	769	4,619	71	6,187
1937-46	15	540	487	2,430	175	3,647
Annual:						
1943-44	0	0	1,271	6,930	53	8,254
1944-45	15	0	1,218	8,061	31	9,325
1945-46	28	1,508	688	7,140	73	9,437
1946-47	34	2,054	187	950	76	3,301
1947-48	27	4,179	98	1,805	26	6,135
1948-49 1/	0	2,883	17	255	37	3,192
Unshelled						
Average:						
1942-46	0	1	5	201	2	209
1937-46	0	1	3	100	1	105
Annual:						
1943-44	0	0	14	425	0	439
1944-45	0	0	11	170	0	181
1945-46	0	0	0	263	5	268
1946-47	0	6	0	145	6	157
1947-48	0	9	0	0	2/	9
1948-49 1/	0	1	0	0	2/	1

1/ 5 months, September through January, 1949 2/ Less than one-half ton.

Compiled from official records of the Bureau of the Census.

The British Ministry of Food has been less active in purchasing nuts than had been anticipated. The prices the British have been willing to pay have been discouragingly low in most countries, and relatively little tonnage was moved. Recent reports have been that the British are contemplating putting nuts on general import licenses, thereby making it possible for private traders to engage again in the business. When this goes into effect it is expected to ease the selling pressure and slow the market in the Mediterranean Basin. There is also some reason to feel that western Germany will enter the markets again in the not-too-distant future for limited quantities at first.

(Continued on Page 249)

C O M M O D I T Y D E V E L O P M E N T S

GRAINS, GRAIN PRODUCTS AND FEEDS

CEYLON'S RICE IMPORTS
GAIN; BELOW PREWAR

Ceylon's rice imports in 1948 amounted to 917 million pounds, a marked gain over 589 million pounds in 1947, according to a report from the American Embassy, Ceylon. Despite the receipt of the largest quantity since the war, imports equaled only 75 percent of prewar average takings of more than 1,200 million pounds annually.

Nearly three-fourths of the 1948 imports originated in Burma, 20 percent in Egypt, 4 percent in Brazil, and 3 percent in Siam. The International Emergency Food Committee's rice allocation for Ceylon during the first half of 1949 is about 520 million pounds, of which the largest proportion is to be imported from Burma. The civil unrest which has retarded shipments from that country in recent months has caused some concern regarding the continued importation of all the allocation.

Total rice imports of about 70 million pounds a month continue to be rationed. Stocks on hand usually amount to about a 3-weeks' supply. The larger of two annual harvests began in the latter part of February, and, despite the occurrence of drought conditions during part of the season, the crop will approximate 550 million pounds in terms of milled rice.

CEYLON: Rice imports by country, average 1935-39, annual 1944-48

Country of origin	Average 1935-1939	1944	1945	1946	1947	1948
	Million pounds	Million pounds	Million pounds	Million pounds	Million pounds	Million pounds
British India..:	191	10	63	43	a/	a/
Burma..........:	794	0	0	17	318	674
Siam...........:	202	0	0	0	0	23
Fr. Indochina..:	23	0	0	0	0	0
Egypt..........:	0	94	218	323	79	181
Brazil.........:	0	133	101	183	177	39
Other countries:	8	14	19	2	15	0
Total.......:	1,218	251	401	568	589	917

a/ Less than 500,000 pounds.

Ceylon Custom Returns.

ITALIAN RICE ACREAGE
ESTIMATE UP

The planted rice acreage of Italy in 1948 equaled 353,000 acres
compared with 325,000 acres in the year before and 362,000 before the
war, according to an official estimate just released. The comparable
production estimate is not yet available. Weather conditions during
the 1948 season, although not quite so favorable as in the preceding
year, were beneficial for the production of high yields per acre.

The Ente Nazionale Risi late in February announced an agreement
to provide rice exports to Bizonia in the amount of 44 million pounds.
The first shipment of 8 million pounds of partially processed rice
was to be made in February. The selling price of this rice was $11.31
per 100 pounds.

FATS AND OILS

U. S. EXPORTS OF
TALLOW INCREASE

Exports of edible and inedible tallow from the United States in 1948
were substantially above those in 1947 and considerably greater than
average exports of prewar years. A total of 69,372,000 pounds of tallow
was exported in 1948. This was one-quarter more than the 55,154,000
pounds shipped out in 1947 and 35 times as great as the 1,961,000 pounds
average for the 1936-39 period. Edible tallow, the bulk of which went
to European countries, was a very minor part of the total exports.

Inedible tallow from the United States, obtainable at lower prices
than in other exporting countries, found a ready market in areas needing
fats for the production of soap and other products. The United States
exported 67,995,000 pounds in 1948. Most of it was sent to European
countries (31,018,000 pounds) and to neighboring countries in North
America including islands of the Caribbean area (29,132,000 pounds).
This represents considerable change from the preceding year in the
destination of shipments. The major part of shipments in 1947 went to
North American countries, with Cuba taking 21,706,000 pounds and Canada
14,132,000 pounds and only 12,366,000 pounds being purchased by
countries in Europe. There were large increases over 1947 and prewar
in the quantities exported in 1948 to the European countries, such as
Belgium-Luxembourg, France, Germany, Italy and Switzerland. Shipments
to the Philippines in 1948 were up sharply from those in 1947, and a
shipment of almost 1,000,000 pounds went to Japan.

Argentina and New Zealand were the other large exporters of tallow
last year. Exports from these 2 countries were 96,800,000 pounds and an
estimated 40,000,000 pounds, respectively.

UNITED STATES: Inedible tallow exports by country of destination
in 1948 with comparisons

Country of destination	Average 1936-39a/	Average 1940-44	1947	1948 b/
	1,000 pounds	1,000 pounds	1,000 pounds	1,000 pounds
NORTH AMERICA				
Canada.................	147	337	14,132	8,650
Costa Rica...	14	23	84	209
Cuba...................	122	3,281	21,706	12,337
Dominican Republic.....	217	197	574	691
Guatemala..............	76	97	280	378
Mexico.................	104	1,031	286	5,163
Panama, Republic of....	35	35	711	1,191
British West Indies....	c/	60	376	304
Others.................	123	151	157	209
Total.............	838	5,212	38,306	29,132
SOUTH AMERICA				
Colombia...............	56	24	794	397
Ecuador................	1	-	117	248
Peru...................	8	17	152	252
Venezuela..............	-	3	534	181
Others.................	11	2	85	52
Total.............	76	46	1,682	1,130
EUROPE				
Belgium-Luxembourg.....	9	-	241	4,651
Finland................	-	299	220	281
France.................	9	-	5,502	10,036
Germany................	10	-	529	3,328
Italy..................	165	2	6	1,482
Netherlands............	17	-	4,554	4,058
Norway.................	18	-	-	220
Switzerland............	115	178	1,221	6,439
Others.................	120	87	93	523
Total.............	463	566	12,366	31,018
ASIA				
Japan..................	116	-	-	972
Philippines, Republic of..	54	-	22	2,361
Others.................	3	3	1	337
Total.............	173	3	23	3,670
AFRICA				
Union of South Africa.....	2	15	2,160	3,044
Others.................	-	10	16	1
Total.............	2	25	2,176	3,045
Grand total...........	1,552	5,852	54,553	67,995

a/ Not separately classified prior to 1936.   b/ Subject to revision.
c/ Less than 500 pounds.

Compiled from official sources.

UNITED STATES: Edible tallow exports by country of destination
in 1948 with comparisons

Country of destination	Average 1935-39	Average 1940-44	1947	1948 a/
	1,000 pounds	1,000 pounds	1,000 pounds	1,000 pounds
NORTH AMERICA				
Canada..........................	13	191	122	120
Cuba............................	168	12	139	43
Mexico..........................	3	44	82	1
Others..........................	25	29	24	63
Total.......................	209	276	367	227
SOUTH AMERICA......................	15	15	48	11
EUROPE				
Austria.........................	b/	b/	-	184
France..........................	-	-	59	-
Greece..........................	-	-	-	100
Netherlands.....................	-	-	116	538
United Kingdom..................	146	202	-	-
Others..........................	30	39	-	254
Total.......................	176	241	175	1,076
Soviet Union....................	-	7,203	-	-
Asia...........................	9	4	11	63
Africa.........................	-	5	-	-
Grand total..................	409	7,744	601	1,377

a/ Subject to revision. b/ Prior to January 1, 1945, Austria included
with Germany.

Compiled from official sources.

U.S. PEANUT EXPORTS
REACH ALL-TIME HIGH

During the calendar year 1948 United States peanut exports reached
the all-time high of 458.7 million pounds, shelled basis; and 10.6
million, unshelled, or a total of almost 700.0 million in terms of
unshelled nuts. This is more than double the total quantity exported
in 1947. As a result of increased peanut production (output has
exceeded 2 billion pounds each year since 1942) the United States has
in recent years become one of the principal exporters. During 1935-39
annual peanut shipments averaged less than 500,000 pounds (unshelled).

Over 82 percent of the 1948 exports of shelled peanuts were sent
to European countries with Germany receiving far more than the total
to all others. Canada was the recipient of over 60 million pounds of
shelled nuts and the largest shipment, 9 million pounds, of unshelled
nuts.

UNITED STATES: Peanut exports, 1948 with comparisons

(1,000 pounds)

Country of destination	Unshelled			Shelled		
	1946	1947a/	1948a/	1946	1947a/	1948a/
orth America:						
Canada.........	2,079:	13,796:	9,364:	32,498:	35,851:	60,340
Cuba...........	381:	601:	8:	410:	11:	15
West Indies.....	113:	264:	432:	61:	169:	151
Others.........	77:	110:	22:	195:	258:	153
Total......	2,650:	14,771:	9,826:	33,164:	36,289:	60,659
outh America	b/ :	607:	136:	27:	36:	133
urope:						
Austria........	- :	- :	- :	506:	- :	61,725
Belgium and						
Luxembourg.....	30:	- :	- :	6:	38,203:	5
Czechoslovakia..	- :	- :	- :	1,806:	- :	6,662
Finland........	- :	- :	- :	b/ :	13,190:	-
France.........	19:	- :	- :	15,761:	45,321:	70,864
Germany........	- :	- :	- :	9:	265:	236,914
Italy..........	b/ :	- :	- :	9:	2,558:	-
Netherlands....	- :	155:	- :	b/ :	48,765:	-
Poland and Danzig	3:	- :	- :	2,626:	16,607:	-
Portugal.......	- :	601:	55:	1:	b/ :	1
Sweden.........	- :	- :	- :	162:	99:	-
Switzerland.....	4,347:	1,423:	577:	701:	5,057:	23
Trieste........	- :	- :	- :	- :	- :	2,214
United Kingdom..	- :	b/ :	- :	5:	4,292:	-
Yugoslavia......	- :	- :	- :	1,001:	1:	-
Others.........	4:	- :	- :	119:	38:	-
Total......	4,403:	2,179:	632:	22,712:	174,396:	378,408
oviet Union	- :	- :	- :	5,040:	- :	-
sia and Oceania:						
Philippines, Re-						
Public of.....	12:	- :	- :	44:	391:	340
Japan..........	- :	- :	- :	- :	962:	1,030
Others.........	- :	- :	- :	19:	16:	12
Total......	12:	- :	- :	63:	1,369:	1,382
frica:						
Algeria........	- :	- :	- :	- :	- :	17,551
Union of South..						
Africa........	- :	1,124:	- :	34:	161:	520
Others.........	1:	- :	- :	3:	2:	2
Total........	1:	1,124:	- :	37:	163:	18,073
Grand total.	7,066:	18,681:	10,594:	61,043:	212,253:	458,655

/ Preliminary. b/ Less than 500 pounds.

ompiled from official sources.

U. S. EXPORTS OF SPECIFIED
FATS, OILS, AND OILSEEDS

The following table shows United States exports of specified fats, oils, and oilseeds during January 1949 with comparisons:

UNITED STATES: Exports of specified fats, oils, and oilseeds, January 1949 with comparisons

Commodity	Unit	Average 1935-39	1947a/	1948a/	January 1948a/	January 1949a/
Soybeans	1,000 bu.	b/ 4,793	2,505	6,497	634	2,087
Soybean oil						
Refined	1,000 lbs.	(6,647	38,883	41,266	9,381	1,858
Crude	" "	(	68,395	41,769	6,627	1,467
Coconut oil						
Refined	" "	3,789	5,491	9,273	1,700	531
Crude	" "	10,442	52,427	9,820	1,035	487
Cottonseed oil						
Refined	" "	4,793	10,977	22,672	11,771	4,572
Crude	" "	1,515	901	10,094	605	2,031
Flaxseed	1,000 bu.	c/	16	1,650	d/	175
Linseed oil	1,000 lbs.	1,280	9,855	29,636	1,226	229
Peanuts						
Shelled	" "	c/{ 452	212,253	458,655	19,111	53,117
Not Shelled	" "	{	18,681	10,594	924	631
Peanut oil, refined	" "	e/ 325	1,579	685	30	4
Cooking fats	" "	2,111	3,594	3,522	362	283
Lard	" "	165,636	380,735	271,835	23,143	33,821
Oleomargarine	" "	180	19,954	3,408	847	158
Tallow						
Edible	" "	c/{1,651	601	1,377	64	-
Inedible	" "	{	54,553	67,995	1,256	13,317

a/ Preliminary.
b/ Average of less than 5 years.
c/ Not separately classified in Foreign Commerce and Navigation.
d/ Less than 500 bushels.
e/ 1939 only.

Compiled from official sources.

U.S. IMPORTS OF SPECIFIED VEGETABLE OIL AND OILSEEDS

The following table shows United States imports of specified vegetable oils and oilseeds during January 1948 with comparisons:

UNITED STATES: Imports a/ of specified oils and oilseeds, January 1949 with comparisons

Commodity	Unit	Average 1935-39	1947 b/	1948 b/	January 1948 b/	January 1949 b/
Babassu kernels	1,000 lbs.	c/	22,233	61,929	5,293	18,057
Babassu oil	" "	d/346	1,747	3,082	220	485
Castor-beans	" "	132,924	276,807	302,511	37,179	35,771
Castor oil	" "	226	6,595	2,441	794	441
Flaxseed	" bu.	18,470	282	1,066	5	58
Linseed oil	" lbs.	713	117,326	3,959	135	e/
Copra	Short tons	230,000	677,660	447,743	56,167	21,824
Coconut oil	1,000 lbs.	342,717	23,559	109,096	11,593	10,049
Oiticica oil	" "	d/7,673	8,471	17,558	463	2,148
Olive oil						
Edible	" "	62,811	11,250	36,093	948	2,671
Inedible	" "	35,448	248	9,775	15	15
Palm oil	" "	321,482	63,212	63,328	5,309	8,448
Sesame seed	" "	58,425	9,479	22,606	1,285	213
Tea seed oil	" "	13,159	6,377	3,601	10	-
Tucum kernels	" "	f/9,810	16,887	11,619	331	1,543
Tung oil	" "	123,190	121,564	133,282	11,053	9,186

a/ Imports for consumption. b/ Preliminary. c/ Not separately classified in Foreign Commerce and Navigation. d/ Average of less than 5 years. e/ Less than 500 pounds. f/ 1939 only.

Compiled from official sources.

PHILIPPINE COPRA EXPORTS IN FEBRUARY LOWER THAN IN FEBRUARY 1948

Philippine Republic copra exports in February totaled 38,700 long tons. This represents a decline of nearly 40 percent from the 63,100 tons shipped in the corresponding month of 1948. Shipments in February were considerably above the small total for January, however, when only 23,800 tons were exported.

The United States was scheduled to receive 13,200 long tons or one-third of the quantity exported from the Republic last month. Over half of this was sent to the Pacific coast with the remainder going to the Atlantic seaboard. Other destinations of shipments included Trieste, France, Italy and Denmark.

Coconut oil exports from the Philippines in February added up to 2,598 long tons. Of this total 2,107 tons were sent to the United States. The remaining 491 tons were shipped to Italy.

PHILIPPINE REPUBLIC: Copra exports, February 1949 with comparisons
(Long tons)

Country a/	Copra distribution				
	Average 1935-39	1948 b/	Jan-Feb 1949 b/	February 1948 b/	1949 b/
United States (total).....	206,801	364,102	33,394	38,214	13,247
Atlantic Coast........	-	61,618	10,297	12,440	6,210
Gulf Coast...........	-	69,320	5,723	4,579	
Pacific Coast........	-	233,164	17,374	21,195	7,037
Canada...................	-	17,049	1,000	2,349	1,000
Costa Rica...............	-	100	-		
Mexico...................	7,260	-	-		
Panama Canal Zone........		707	320	407	-
Panama, Republic of......	-	1,357	209	-	-
Colombia.................	-	6,995		-	
Venezuela................	-	3,868	1,133	-	
Austria..................	-	6,000	-	-	
Belgium..................	10	1,000	-	-	-
Denmark..................	6,025	26,536	3,000	7,634	3,000
France...................	24,589	65,912	6,507	14,544	5,050
Bizonal Germany..........	7,309	17,250	2,914	-	2,914
Italy....................	4,079	21,900	3,994	-	3,994
Netherlands..............	28,415	8,944	1,050	-	1,050
Norway...................	91	9,276	2,400	-	2,400
Poland...................	-	31,749	-	-	-
Sweden...................	4,183	4,748	-	-	-
Switzerland..............	-	1,000	-	-	-
Japan....................	1,047	24,339	-	-	-
Syria....................		1,443	-	-	-
Egypt....................	1,271	-	-	-	-
Union of South Africa....	-	-	512	-	-
Others...................	8,758 c/	11,350 c/	6,000 c/	-	c/ 6,000
Total..........	299,838	625,630	62,433	63,148	38,655

a/ Declared destination.   b/ Preliminary.   c/ Temporary destination Trieste.

American Embassy, Manila.

INDIA'S COCONUT SHORTAGE SERIOUSLY
AFFECTING ITS SOAP INDUSTRY

Production of coconuts and coconut oil in India has failed to keep pace with the sharply increasing demands of the Indian soap industry. The shortage of domestic supplies has become more apparent in recent months because of difficulties in obtaining adequate supplies from Ceylon. Extremely high prices for coconut oil have made it difficult for the soap industry to meet competitive prices for soap. In December coconut oil prices in Cochin ranged from 1,918 to 2,016 rupees ($575 to $605) per long ton, an increase of nearly 50 percent from the corresponding prices in 1947.

The growing per capita consumption of soap, together with a rapidly expanding population, has necessitated increased imports of copra and coconut oil into India since 1930. The per capita consumption of soap prior to World War I is estimated to have been only 4 ounces. This had increased to 8 ounces by the time World War II had ended. Current estimates of consumption are 12 ounces per person and expectations are that this will rise to 16 ounces within the next 5 years.

MALAYAN PALM-OIL EXPORTS IN 1948
GREATER THAN YEAR BEFORE

British Malaya exported 48,811 long tons of palm oil in 1948. About 96 percent of this quantity, which exceeded total shipments in 1947 by 3,480 tons, was purchased by the United Kingdom.

December exports of palm oil, sent to the United Kingdom, Italy, Egypt and Syria, totaled 4,356 long tons. This was nearly one-fourth less than the 5,705 tons shipped out in the preceding month. Of the total shipments in December, 2,335 tons were from the Federation of Malaya. The balance came from Singapore.

Exports of palm kernels from Malaya in 1948 came to 6,472 long tons, an increase of 23 percent over the total for 1947. Nearly 70 percent was sent to the United Kingdom. France purchased 20 percent of the total and the balance was bought by the Netherlands.

There were 818 long tons of palm kernels shipped from Malaya in December. All of this, 317 tons more than the quantity exported in the preceding month, was sent to France.

TROPICAL PRODUCTS

CEYLON'S 1949 TEA PRODUCTION FORECAST
SLIGHTLY LARGER; EXPORTS INCREASE

Ceylon's tea production for the calendar year 1949 has been forecast at 294 million pounds. This compares with approximately 276 million pounds in 1948, 299 million pounds in 1947, and the 1935-39 average of 232 million pounds, according to a report from the American Embassy in Colombo.

million pounds as compared with 287 million pounds in 1947, 292 million pounds in 1946, and an annual average of 222 million pounds during the period 1935-39. There were no recorded exports of green tea from Ceylon during 1948. The total value of 1948 tea exports is reported at about 590 million rupees (178 million dollars) as compared with an annual average of 164 million rupees (60 million dollars) during the prewar years 1935-39. Ceylon exported about 98 million pounds of tea to the United Kingdom in 1948, as compared with 108 million pounds in 1947 and 149 million pounds in 1946. The United States was Ceylon's second best customer, importing about 42 million pounds of Ceylon tea in 1948 as compared with 21 million pounds in 1947 and 45 million pounds in 1946.

Ronald C. Brooks, Vice President of the Ceylon Association in London and Chairman of the International Tea Committee, while in Colombo in October, 1948, stated that the outlook for Ceylon tea was doubtful. He said that unless early attempts are made to reduce tea production costs in Ceylon, reduce taxes on tea, and to re-open London auctions, Ceylon teas would not regain their prewar reputation for good quality at fair prices. He expressed the view that if these steps are not taken, the Island's tea industry might be seriously jeopardized.

The Ceylon Government is reported to have proposed to the United Kingdom a renewal of the tea contract which expired in December, 1948 and re-opening of auction sales. The new contract would provide for bulk sales of a large part of the 1949 crop to the British Ministry of Food. Auction sales in Colombo and London would be re-opened for the disposal of quantities which are not sold through bulk sales.

COLOMBIA'S 1948-49 COFFEE CROP
LOWER; 1948 EXPORTS HIGHER

Colombia's 1948-49 coffee crop is now expected to be about 3 percent below the 1947-48 crop. Exports during 1948 were 5 percent above 1947 according to the American Embassy in Bogota.

Weather conditions in Colombia have been generally favorable for the 1948-49 coffee crop, and the quality of coffee being dried is reported very good. It is now thought that exportable coffee from the 1948/49 crop (July to June) will amount to about 5,650,000 bags of 60 kilograms. This is slightly below the 1947/48 exportable production of 5,840,000 bags but substantially above the 1935/36-1939/40 average of 4,202,000 bags.

Colombia's 1948 coffee exports of approximately 5,588,000 bags shows an increase over the 1947 exports of 5,339,000 bags but was still slightly below the 1946 record high of 5,662,000 bags. Dollar returns from 1948 coffee exports were $198,000,000 as compared with $168,000,000 in 1947 and $138,000,000 in 1946.

Coffee stocks at Colombian ports on January 15, 1949 were reported as 401,000 bags compared with 408,000 bags on January 10, 1948 and 417,000 bags on January 15, 1947. No statistics are available regarding quantity of stocks in the interior, but it is believed that these stocks now are increasing because of the drop in New York coffee prices. It is estimated that almost 450,000 bags of coffee are consumed in Colombia each year. No coffee is used for other than beverage purposes and none is destroyed. About two-thirds of local consumption is made from black, broken or other beans which are below export quality.

COLOMBIA: Exports of green coffee in 1948, with comparisons

Destination	Average		1946	1947 a/	1948 a/
	1935-39	1940-44			
	1,000 bags	1,000 bags	1,000 bags	1,000 bags	1,000 bags
United States	3,060	4,193	5,257	4,983	5,215
Other Western Hemisphere	150	115	215	176	177
Europe	761	38	175	163	160
Other	2	21	15	17	36
Total	3,973	4,367	5,662	5,339	5,588

a/ Preliminary.

Official statistics and U. S. foreign service reports.

No census of the number of coffee trees in Colombia has been taken, but the number has been estimated to be about 800 million trees. This figure is based on informal information received from the National Federation of Coffee Growers that the average Colombian coffee tree produces about 1 pound of milled coffee per year.

COTTON AND OTHER FIBER

COTTON TEXTILE PRODUCTION INCREASING
IN WESTERN GERMANY

The German cotton textile industry made remarkable gains in production since the Bizonal currency reform June 20, 1948.

Yarn production in Bizonal Germany increased from 15.6 million pounds in June 1948 to 24.9 million pounds in October 1948. This would indicate that the mills there are consuming from 50,000 to 60,000 bales of cotton a month, which is nearly double the monthly rate during the 1947-48 season. Production leveled off somewhat in the fourth quarter of 1948 but with the arrival of ample cotton supplies since the turn of the year, production has made further gains with the trend still upward.

The most important effects of the monetary reform itself were to release hoarded stocks of raw material and finished products, improve labor
efficiency, and raise the morale of the entire population of Western
Germany. The release of hoarded goods and increased production have filled
long-empty shelves and improved the food supply situation. The upward
trend in prices has also come to a halt.

Labor productivity is now some 20 or 30 percent higher than in 1947,
and this will be maintained if the situation in regard to prices, wages,
and food remains steady. However, until technical efficiency of the machinery can be improved there is little hope of any further increase in
labor efficiency in the near future. The textile plants urgently need
long overdue repairs and replacements. The general labor supply is expected to be ample although there is need for additional skilled workers
in the industry.

Uncertain supplies of raw cotton, shortages of skilled labor and fuel,
and the fact that much of the machinery is damaged, worn, and obsolete
have been the main obstacles in increasing cotton production. However,
most of these difficulties have now been overcome to some extent.

Work stoppage due to shortage of raw cotton has become less frequent
this season as ample supplies of raw cotton are now reaching Western
Germany. The Bizone has 3 sources of funds for the procurement of cotton.
First are Army funds for the prevention of disease and unrest. There is
little need now, however, for the use of these funds for the procurement
of cotton. The other 2 sources are the Economic Cooperation Administration
funds and proceeds from the export of German products. Since October 1948
the major part of German cotton supplies has been financed by ECA. Through
January 31, 1949, ECA had authorized the procurement of 280,600 bales of
United States cotton for the Bizone and 77,500 bales for the French Zone.
About 60 percent of this cotton had been shipped by the end of January 1949.
The United States has supplied most of the cotton Western Germany has consumed since World War II and in the first 6 months of the current season
has supplied practically all cotton it has imported. The United States in
the first 6 months of the present season exported 272,000 bales of cotton
to Western Germany which now ranks as one of the most important markets for
American cotton.

Although the cotton textile industry has made a remarkable recovery,
production is still below prewar. The demand for textiles is still strong
and production can hardly meet day-to-day requirements much less catch up
with the backlog of accumulated demand. Rationing and price controls are
still strictly maintained in Western Germany. German consumers are reported to be getting between 40 and 50 percent of the Bizone production.
A large share of the German textile production is exported as a direct
means of acquiring foreign exchange needed for the procurement of raw
cotton.

(Text continued on Page 249)

ON-PRICE QUOTATIONS
OREIGN MARKETS

The following table shows certain cotton-price quotations on foreign markets
erted at current rates of exchange:

COTTON: Spot prices in certain foreign markets, and the
U.S. gulf-port average

Market location, kind, and quality	Date 1949	Unit of weight	Unit of currency	Price in foreign currency	Equivalent U.S. cents per pound
andria		:Kantar			
mouni, Good............:	3-17	: 99.05 lbs.	:Tallari	47.35	39.51
mouni, F.G.F...........:	"	"	"	45.35	37.84
nak, Good.............:	"	"	"	78.35	65.38
nak, F.G.F............:	"	"	"	68.35	57.03
ay		:Candy			
ila, Fine.............:	"	: 784 lbs.	:Rupee	620.00	23.86
ach, Fine.............:	"	"	"	650.00	25.01
pala, East African.....:	"	"	"	(not	available)
chi		:Maund			
Punjab, S.G., Fine.....:	3-16	: 82.28 lbs.	"	87.50	32.08
F Sind, S.G., Fine.....:	"	"	"	96.80	35.49
F Punjab, S.G., Fine...:	"	"	"	98.00	35.93
os Aires		:Metric ton			
e B...................:	3-17	: 2204.6 lbs.	:Peso	a/3350.00	45.24
a		:Sp. quintal			
guis, Type 5..........:	3-16	: 101.4 lbs.	:Sol	b/ (not	quoted)
a, Type 1.............:	"	"	"	b/ (not	quoted)
fe		:Arroba			
a, Type 4.............:	3-17	: 33.07 lbs.	:Cruzeiro	215.00	35.37
tao, Type 5...........:	"	"	"	215.00	35.37
Paulo					
Paulo, Type 5.........:	"	"	"	202.00	33.23
eon		:Sp. quintal			
ling, 15/16"..........:	"	: 101.4 lbs.	:Peso	192.00	27.18
ton-Galveston-New					
eans av. Mid. 15/16"...:	"	:Pound	:Cent	XXXXX	32.50

ations of foreign markets reported by cable from U.S. Foreign Service posts
ad. U.S. quotations from designated spot markets.
Nominal
Omitted from last week's table: Lima, March 9, 1949, not available.

1948 MID-SEASON ALMOND REPORT--(Continued from Page 235)

Early in the season it was anticipated by many that because of a small Italian olive oil output, almonds and hazelnuts would again be used for oil. The Italian Government has made arrangements to import vegetable oils, and to this writing there has been no report of nuts being crushed for oil. The world markets at present are rather slow. It is not expected that a strong export will develop for the remainder of the season. The United States has recently purchased limited quantities of bar-type almonds in Italy, and it appears now that small lots of this type will continue to be purchased for the remainder of the season.

WORLD EGG PRODUCTION--- (Continued from Page 232)

Contrary to earlier trade estimates, the 1948 chicken hatch in Argentina was not more than 5 percent above the 1947 hatch, notwithstanding a favorable egg-feed price relationship. Feed prices to poultrymen may be higher in 1949 but the current price of chickens and eggs is the highest ever recorded in Argentina. This indicates a strong consumer demand and exports of eggs and chickens are apt to be small as the world price level of eggs and poultry, in comparison with present Argentine prices, is not favorable to exports.

This is one of a series of regularly scheduled reports on world agricultural production approved by the Office of Foreign Agricultural Relations Committee on Foreign Crop and Livestock Statistics. For this report, the Committee was composed of Joseph A. Becker, Chairman, C. M. Purves, Floyd E. Davis, Karen J. Friedmann, Constance H. Farnworth, and Stanley Mehr.

COTTON AND OTHER FIBER
(Continued from Page 247)

It is estimated that about 83 percent of the available spindles were active in the latter part of 1948. Also, there are about 1,000,000 additional spindles that can be put into operation when repaired. The present program plans full use of existing spindle capacity and putting back in operation most of the spindles requiring repair. The Bizone Government plans to raise cotton consumption by 1952 almost to the 1936 level of 840,000 bales.

How long it will take to replace or repair these spindles depends on how fast new machinery and parts can be turned out. The output of textile machinery has been greatly increased but is still far below requirements. There must be some adjustment in the industry to compensate for the cessation of trade with Eastern Germany.

Consumption requirements in the Bizone for the 1949-50 season have been estimated at 680,000 bales, which is about equal to the present rate. This would indicate that even assured ample supplies of raw cotton the limiting factor in the near future may be inability to expand present mill capacity.

Lightning Source UK Ltd.
Milton Keynes UK
UKHW012036040219
336748UK00009B/1371/P